The Art of UnLearning

VOLUME 4

TOP EXPERTS SHARE

PERSONAL STORIES
OF MOVING FROM
TRAGEDY TO TRIUMPH

The Art of UnLearning

VOLUME 4

TOP EXPERTS SHARE

PERSONAL STORIES OF MOVING FROM TRAGEDY TO TRIUMPH

DIVYA PAREKH & LISA MARIE PEPE

The Art of UnLearning Volume 4: From Tragedy to Triumph

Copyright © 2020 Divya Parekh and Lisa Marie Pepe

All rights reserved.

ISBN-13: 978-1-949513-20-2

The DP Group, LLC

No part of this book may be reproduced in any form or by any electronic or mechanical means, including information storage and retrieval systems, without written permission from the author, except for the use of brief quotations in a book review.

GET PUBLISHED

To receive your free gift and see how you, too, can become a published author, email us at info@getpublishedwithus.com.

DEDICATION

This book is dedicated to women entrepreneurs across the globe. We are also thrilled to share that the proceeds of the sales of this book (minus our expenses) will be donated to Kiva. Kiva.org is an international nonprofit, founded in 2005 and based in San Francisco, with a mission to connect people through lending to alleviate poverty.

Kiva celebrates and supports people looking to create a better future for themselves, their families, and their communities. By giving as little as $25 to Kiva, anyone can help a borrower start or grow a business, go to school, access clean energy, or realize their potential. For some, it's a matter of survival; for others, it's the fuel for a lifelong ambition (Referenced from https://www.kiva.org/work-with-us/fellows).

The profits of this book (minus our expenses) go straight to Kiva, and once there, 100% of every dollar goes to funding loans. Kiva covers administrative costs primarily through voluntary donations, as well as through support from grants and sponsors.

We can't tell you how excited we are to be supporting a lot of people's dreams because of this book!

Divya Parekh and Lisa Marie Pepe

INTRODUCTION

Life is a series of ups and downs filled with peaks and valleys. Each of us experiences our own unique journey and sometimes the path we choose turns into a dead end or a roadblock. Plain and simple — we all have obstacles that seem to appear out of nowhere, but it's not about how many times we get knocked down. It's about how many times we get back up that matters most. How we overcome life's adversities is what defines us!

In *The Art of Unlearning: From Tragedy to Triumph* are the stories of six gifted women who have experienced a myriad of adversities and a bonus chapter on living the life you want. While the circumstances are different for each author, as are the solutions they've chosen, the common thread that binds them together is their ability to rise up and meet the challenges they've faced. Yes! Every woman in this collection of stories made a conscientious decision to fight her way out of her own personal darkness and into the light.

The stories you'll read in this anthology follow a powerful theme — women facing and overcoming insurmountable struggles, adversities, and personal setbacks. While these women now work actively today with other women in various ways, they believe their stories can serve as a guide for others. They know that in sharing these very personal narratives that they can serve as role models to others who may be facing similar obstacles. It is their hope that in sharing how they've overcome such obstacles, those who read their stories will find their own courage and strength to rise up and overcome their own obstacles.

You might see yourself in one of the stories, or pieces of yourself in all of them. Take from these stories what you find beneficial to your situation. As each of these women shows, it takes perseverance to move through whatever tough times you are experiencing. Learn from them. Most of all, allow yourself to find hope and encouragement.

This is the fourth anthology in *The Art of Unlearning Series* from the creators of *Make Your Message a Movement*. We encourage professionals and entrepreneurs to achieve their highest potential and crush their goals by building and nurturing relationships. One of our core philosophies is the idea that a powerful book is an incredible launch pad to creating a successful, sustainable, and impactful business.

As part of our philosophy that we all need to give back to nurture and sustain human connectivity, the profits from this book are going to Kiva — an organization that helps with crowdfunding loans and unlocking capital for the underserved, improving the quality and cost of financial services, and addressing the underlying barriers to financial access around the world. Through Kiva's work, students can pay for tuition, women can start businesses, farmers can invest in equipment and families can afford needed emergency care. Check them out on www.kiva.org.

Sit back and enjoy the heartwarming and thought-provoking stories from these extraordinary women. Their courage is contagious.

Divya Parekh and Lisa Marie Pepe
info@getpublishedwithus.com

CONTENTS

DEDICATION	vii
INTRODUCTION	ix
From Quadriplegic To Hiking Over 500 Miles	1
Courtney Runyon	
Shhh, Secrets, Don't Tell	25
Elizabeth Lupacchino	
From Victim to Victor	35
Kristi Van Sickle	
The Tightrope of Ghosting Yourself	45
Janis Melillo	
The Leader in You	55
Sherry Wurgler	
Embracing Vision	65
Toni Jo Beck	
Living The Life You Want	77
Divya Parekh	
ABOUT THE ART OF UNLEARNING FOUNDERS	97
Divya Parekh and Lisa Marie Pepe	

"We fall in love with what we have, or we fall apart."

Courtney Runyon

STORY 1

From Quadriplegic To Hiking Over 500 Miles

Courtney Runyon

Shit. After 7 months of learning to walk again, I was already back on the ground and couldn't stand.

My knee was throbbing and I was in a foreign country, alone in the woods, on the side of a rocky mountain. It was blazing hot and the only water I had on me was the glitter of sweat dancing down my forehead. My frizzy, tangled hair was a few hours away from twirling into Medusa, and nature's premier makeup artist, the sun, had already brushed fiery red all over my face.

I had slipped on God's pile of stoned marbles and fell right into another one of His perfectly orchestrated booby traps, flat on my back.

It was only the first day.

Hiking 500 miles on the Camino De Santiago across northern Spain first made its debut on my radar in 2013. I was traveling on a yearlong sabbatical through 27 countries on 6 continents, after quitting my corporate career, and selling everything I owned at the carefree, healthy age of 28 years old.

I ate. I prayed. I loved.

But it wasn't until December of 2017 the Camino trekked its way to the number one spot on my bucket list.

I was an adult in a diaper — both figuratively and literally. Breathing was hard and when I spoke, I sounded like Darth Vader after a rock concert and 3 packs of Marlboro Red cigarettes. Because I hadn't walked in months, the muscles in my body were not there to cushion my bones. The pressure on the thin layer of skin separating my bones from the bed felt like a finger shut in a car door. I hadn't slept through the night in weeks. Every 45 minutes I woke up in excruciating pain and had to buzz the nurses to come and roll me to my side for relief. I had been under anesthesia four times, and had more blood sucked out of me in those 14 days in the hospital than Sookie Stackhouse did by vampires in the entire first season of "True Blood.

My skin looked pale gray like a vampire…

I was sneaky. I only drank liquids when the nurses weren't looking, so my water privileges wouldn't be taken away. My stomach muscles were too weak to cough out the water my throat was too weak to swallow, so I often lay there choking. I couldn't even sneeze when my nose itched, but you get used to itching and not being able to scratch it when you can't move your arms.

The hospital bed alarm sounded like Jim Carey's "most annoying sound in the world" from "Dumb & Dumber" anytime someone sat on the bed. I couldn't sit up or roll over, so I spent months sleeping unwillingly on my back. I rarely got to go outside, and when I did, it was to sit for 15 minutes in a nursing home parking lot.

I was trapped in my own body, with little to do but stare at the white walls stained yellow by a revolving door of sad stories over the years and grieve the loss of all the things on my bucket list I never got to do.

I always wanted to run a marathon.

I never tried.

I promised myself one day I would backpack through Italy with the love of my life.

I never did.

I talked about hiking the Camino de Santiago across northern Spain.

I never went.

And all of the sudden I couldn't run, walk, or hike. I had new dreams.

Walk on the beach during sunset without falling down. Get up out of the bed to use the bathroom without being draped over someone's arm. And run my fingers through my hair when it got in my face.

When things were at their worst, I was so desperate to escape the discomfort of my own body, I'd close my eyes, picture myself dancing on the beach in a red dress, and fantasize about what it would feel like to be on my feet again with the sand between my toes, the wind through my hair, and the sun on my skin.

I dreamt of all the things I already had before I got sick.

I was so happy and healthy before. I had a great job, the best friends in the world, traveled often, and I was madly in love. I drank organic green smoothies for breakfast, home cooked vegan meals for dinner, worked out 6 days a week, and meditated every day. I even used to do a guided meditation practicing gratitude for the ability to walk.

I was so confident.

I had a light inside of me, a fire even, and could project it out through my eyes like lasers with a warm smile, or out my mouth with some type of quick-witted comment or sincere complimentary charm.

I. LOVED. MY. LIFE.

And I lived it to the fullest. No moment passed untouched by my zest for life or curious sense of wonder. I dreamed. I planned. I changed my plans. And once the stress of work calmed down and my boyfriend's financial situation stabilized, we were going to finally move out of Vegas and go and live the life we always talked about. There was so much I wanted to do. The world was a playground, and everything was a possibility — until it wasn't.

My mom had always told me her early 30s were her favorite time in life. It made me sad to think mine would be wasted working on "getting my life back," so I had a decision to make. I was a 33-year-old girl paralyzed from the neck down. I could either be sad about the life I lost, or create a bad ass life with the one I was given.

That day in the hospital, I promised myself I would do all the things I was too busy to do before. I'd go to Spain, walk the Camino De Santiago, and travel the world as soon as I was strong enough. Having this vision brought my spirit to life. My future is what got me out of bed in the morning, into therapy every day, and back up off the floor after every time I fell — but I wasn't getting better.

I was getting worse.

After nine long months of endless test, doctor appointments, pinches and pokes, the doctors diagnosed me with an autoimmune disorder called chronic inflammatory demyelinating polyneuropathy — aka "CIDP." But I was declining so rapidly and I was so resistant to treatment, the doctors didn't even know if they had diagnosed me accurately. When I was discharged from the hospital, the incredible medical team had tested and treated me with everything they possibly could, but there was nothing else they could do. Even the rehab hospital denied me, because I lacked any signs of potential improvement, so I was going home to wait and see if I got better —

Or if I got worse.

I was defeated, hanging on by a thread, and finally ready to surrender to the one thing I had been too scared to try. As I searched myself, I knew, *you can't heal in the same environment that made you sick.*

I had to say goodbye.

When my symptoms first started almost 12 months prior, my three greatest stressors were my boyfriend, my job, and living the Las Vegas lifestyle.

My mind had been telling me to move out of Vegas, but I didn't, because I loved my life.

My body had been telling me to focus on my needs instead of the needs of my partner, but I sacrificed my health to try and make my boyfriend happy, because I loved him so deeply.

My soul had been telling me to follow my passions, but I stayed in my stressful job, because I loved the people.

I had already gone on disability a few months before and it was disheartening. It's a strange feeling to admit you can no longer work, but on August 18 of 2017, I finally made the call when I couldn't lift my arms to reach the computer and my voice was so weak it made talk to text impossible.

For the next 7 weeks that followed, I poured all my energy into healing. Infrared saunas, red light therapy, chiropractic, PEMF, acupuncture, Nutritional IV therapy, ozone, chelation, colonics, the AIP diet, and almost $20,000 in different doctors, supplements, and protocols — but nothing seemed to slow down the progression.

My boyfriend started disappearing in and out of opportunities to numb himself from reality, sometimes reappearing with an after party in our living room, and every day that passed without either of us working, my health grew weaker, our financial situation tighter, and our fights stronger. I needed him to work full time, but I needed his full time care. It was a lose-lose. I was depending on someone I couldn't depend on and he was taking care of someone he couldn't take care of AND work at the same time.

I had to get out of there. I had to get away from the stress.

When I finally rolled out of my condo in Vegas on October 9 of 2017 to go to the rehab hospital in California, I still had my lotion and toothbrush on my side of the sink for when I returned.

But I never came home.

I never saw that condo again.

On December 20, 2017 — the day I was discharged from the hospital with little to no hope — there was one stressor I was still clinging my motionless nails into.

I called my boyfriend — my partner in crime, best friend, and biggest fan — and through my chapped lips and runny nose (I couldn't lift my arm to wipe), I found the words I never thought I'd say.

I let him go.

He was the love of my life.

And I started improving 2 days later.

It wasn't until I shed the weight of what was

no longer serving me, I truly started to heal. I was never going to make it to the other side of my autoimmune as long as I held onto the baggage weighing me down with paralyzing stress. Las Vegas, my ex, and the career I worked so hard for — I had to leave them behind so I could move forward.

Our immune system's job is to protect our health and eliminate what is harmful. My immune system took away my ability to walk, talk, and work, forcing me out of an unhealthy, stressful environment.

It did its job.

I was finally on the upswing. After 12 months of declining and months without being able to lift a finger or wiggle a toe, I moved my right arm … and then my left foot. The new medication suddenly started working, my nerves started waking up, and the rehab hospital finally let me in — but at the end of the day, I had lost my home, career, boyfriend, and life as I knew it. I still couldn't dress, feed, bathe, or wipe myself.

On the first day of the rehab hospital, the therapist wheeled me out into the therapy gym and parked me by a fold out table, where I waited for my evaluation. The walls were white and they had the markings of an old building. My yellow hospital socks were three sizes too big and dangled off my toes.

I felt numb.

It was one of those days I just wanted to listen to Coldplay, Dave Matthews, or some other familiar, semi sappy kind of music that mellowed me out. I wanted to be alone. Either completely alone or surrounded by strangers. I didn't want to be asked how my day was or have an awkward exchange about the weather. All I wanted was a moment of peaceful stillness while the dust of my feelings settled.

I knew I was in there somewhere, but I was hidden under a straitjacket in a paralyzed body bag. My life had become unrecognizable. I couldn't help but look around the surroundings of my new "arm and leg school," and feel like a foreign student. Stroke patients. Amputees. Brain injuries. And everyone was so old.

I didn't belong there.

Loss. So much loss.

I had lost days at the beach and days at the lake. Warm showers in the morning and long walks on a nice day. Going to friends' birthday parties and going to see my favorite band. Cooking in the kitchen and swimming in the pool. Dancing to music and driving to work.

I had lost almost everything.

I was staring down at the table with a lifeless expression, zoning out the uncomfortable moans and groans of the other patients when I heard her laugh. She was an older Asian woman with a beautiful smile. Her children were visiting her during therapy and when I locked eyes with her it hit me.

I am so much more the person she was being than the person I was being.

That day was a turning point for me. I had the nurse wheel me back to my room, fished out a pair of pink fuzzy costume ears someone had given me, and put them on. The rest of the day every single person that saw me either laughed or smiled, which in turn made me laugh or smile.

Happiness is a funny thing. It can be the master of disguise or a seemingly hidden treasure — but looking for happiness is like looking for your phone when it's in your hand. It's never lost or out of reach and once you double check what you already have, you'll find what you thought you were missing.

When we are suffering, our "happy place" seems out of reach or a thing of the past, but being happy or grateful is not a destination. Gratitude is a torch you can turn on at any moment to shed light on hope, happiness, and joy.

We fall in love with what we have, or we fall apart. Our thoughts, our actions, our intentions

… they're the oxygen that brings our soul to life, or the poison that kills it.

I spent a total of 108 days and nights in different hospitals and nursing homes, and I fell in love with it. I turned my rooms into an oasis of essential oils and music you'd hear in a fancy spa. I brought in my own refrigerator of organic paleo food, a tea kettle, and a blender. As my costume collection grew, I started filming myself in therapy and then consolidated them into music videos. Because I couldn't use my hands to write, I used my nose to type on the keyboard of my phone and it's funny how accurate I am.

I shared a little on social media. I shared more. I shared it all, and what happened next was unexpected. As I continued to vulnerably open up and post my wins, my losses, and everything in between so publicly, I received an inpour of support from friends, family, and complete strangers.

A revolving door of gifts and visitors circled my hospital bed. Some of them I knew. Some of them I didn't. Thousands and thousands of dollars were donated for treatment and a meal train kept my parents' fridge full for weeks. My nails never went long without a manicure, nor my face long without a facial or a little makeup.

I got help popping my pimples and itching my back. Brushing my hair and rubbing my feet.

Family laughed with me. Friends slept beside me. And some strangers even cried with me. My support system became my arms where I couldn't reach, my legs when I couldn't walk, and my voice when I couldn't speak.

I saw the best side of people every day I sat in that wheelchair. People are good, but until you learn to be vulnerable and be a good receiver, your support system doesn't stand a chance to show you what they're made of. The flood of love kept me uplifted and connected with people, instead of feeling isolated and alone.

I felt happy.

I was happy and it showed. Messages started flooding my inbox daily from people telling me how much following my story, watching my videos, and reading my words had changed their life and perspective for the better. Seeing the joy on my face from a wheelchair gave them the courage they needed to quit feeling sorry for themselves and accept their own life with humor and grace. My story even made it on the news, which later went on to win an Emmy.

There is no such thing as a perfect life or "getting your life back." You still have your life until you are dead, and life only exists in the present moment — so have fun with it.

I had lost the life I loved, but by letting go of it,

I found so much love, joy, meaning, and purpose in the life I was living. I was done waiting on a boyfriend to be ready, a job to be steady, or for all of the stars to align, sparkling down on me like confetti to live the life of my dreams.

After 7 months in a wheelchair, 15 months learning to walk, and countless tears, my mom and sister took me to the beach, I stepped foot on the sand, and even though I could not zip it myself, I danced in my red dress with the wind in my hair, and the sun on my skin.

Before I could put on my own shoes, I went to Mexico — twice — and as soon as my hands were strong enough to tie my own shoelaces, I was hanging off the back of an ATV, off roading through the jungle of Costa Rica. I spent 21 days traveling through Guatemala solo to learn yoga before I could stand on one foot (or brush my own hair), and before I could even drive a car, I found myself boating in the pacific. I spent 21 days backpacking through Morocco before I could close my own suitcase, and before I could run, I booked a flight to Spain to go on the 500-mile hike that had been collecting dust at the top of my bucket list for far too long.

On the day I slipped and fell on God's marbles on the Camino De Santiago, I was scared. I questioned what I had gotten myself into and challenged the intuition of my own heart — but God doesn't lose his marbles. Just because we stumble over a bump in the road, it doesn't mean we are on the wrong path. Had I not fallen on my first day of hiking the Camino, I wouldn't have met the two Englishmen and the Irishman who found me with a bum covered in red dirt and offered their hand to escort me down the mountain — my Camino Angels.

As soon as the heartbeat in my knee quit thumping, we locked arms and walked down the yellow pebble road like the Wizard of Oz to safety. 500 miles, 35 days, and thousands of pebbles later, I crossed the finish line with my Camino Angels, my best friend, and my cousin by my side.

I had fulfilled my greatest dream, but It didn't look the way I had always envisioned it. When I first heard of the Camino, I always pictured a strong girl, ready to take on the world at the end — not the disabled woman who fell on the first day of it. But if I hadn't gotten autoimmune, I wouldn't have broken up with my boyfriend or gone on disability. I wouldn't have had the time or the fire inside of me to actually go do it. I wouldn't have fallen and met the Englishman who would later help me create the business I've always wanted and couldn't have built without him.

I didn't plan on getting paralyzed, but because I did, I'm living my best life.

It is not our job to plan every detail of our life or control our circumstances. It is our job to set intentions, manifest, have faith, and believe in our wildest dreams — and then let God do the rest.

We are not the artist of this world.

We are part of the art.

But it's still hard to let go sometimes. I'm 35, legally disabled, and live with my parents.

I do miss my old life. I miss seeing the mountains every morning through my window and entertaining friends who came to stay with us. I miss walking into a room feeling sexy and free, instead of wobbly, stiff, and misshapen. I miss companionship and playing with someone's hair. I miss dancing. I miss being able to express my free Spirit.

I used to move my body in so many ways that I can't now, and I've been trapped behind the limitations of this body for so long.

Today I'm limited.

Every single step is hard, and to use my hands is even harder.

I was so full of life before and had so much to offer.

But you can't have the good parts of every phase of life at the same time.

One day I will look back on this time in my life and miss it.

I'll miss watching an episode of "Vikings" every night with my parents.

I'll miss walking to downtown McKinney every other day to my favorite coffee shop or doing a winetasting with a friend at the wine bar with the local farm boy playing guitar.

The farmers market… I'll miss every little thing about it.

I'll miss being able to live stress-free and heal, because not working freed up every hour of the day for self-care.

I'll miss being my sister's third child, learning how to walk with my baby nephew, and I already miss being fed.

(I am amusingly the only paralyzed person I know that enjoyed being fed, but it always made me feel so loved, cared for, and daintily fragile.)

I'll miss surprising everyone I meet abroad by traveling solo with disabilities.

It makes me laugh every time.

I'll miss all of the times my friends, family, and strangers shared their love so deeply and sincerely.

I'll miss feeling life so intensely.

I'll miss having no strings attached to a relationship, career, or a specific identity.

The truth is I'm more free today than I ever have been. Every choice I make of every day is because I want to, not because I have to.

Everything I own can fit into a suitcase, and when the day comes, I can take the suitcase anywhere in the world to start over.

I get to fall in love all over again, and maybe even get married.

The fact that some of the best days of my life haven't happened yet excites me.

Which is why I can miss my old life and not wish I was still in it.

Why I can be excited for my future, but not in a rush to get to it.

You cannot have all of the good moments in your life all at once.

You can't have every amazing experience you'll ever have in one day.

It's not possible.

I had to say goodbye to my life in Vegas to be able to receive the gifts of my life here in Texas, and one day I'll have to say goodbye to seeing my dad's eternally optimistic grin every morning and my mom's heart-melting hugs every night to receive the gifts of the next chapter of my story.

The good things in our life are sprinkled throughout every phase of our time on earth, and we are meant to enjoy them as they come, in the moment, as they happen right in front of us.

Once they pass, let them go. Miss them even.

But live in the present. Because one day you're going to miss something from your life today.

Enjoy it while it's here.

Because the joy of today could be gone tomorrow.

What gifts do you already have that you can appreciate today?

What dreams do you have for the future?

Go chase them. Don't leave them on the back burner until it's too late.

Sometimes our dreams seem so far away we get overwhelmed, confused, and lost before we even give them a chance.

We give up.

The people who succeed know this secret.

Our greatest victories are built on baby steps.

Just take your first step … And then the next and then another one. Don't overwhelm yourself. Keep putting one foot in front of the other.

You are a happy, loving, beautiful, and amazing person. That is who you are and if you don't feel that way then you are just trapped.

Whatever you're going through, you CAN do it!!!

…AND be happy!

Every single day we can have a small victory.

Take things one at a time until one day you look up and you are exactly where you want to be.

Life isn't about waiting for the storm to pass; it's learning to dance in a red dress in the sand.

Special Gift

"I know healing from trauma is hard, and staying positive can be even harder. Please feel free to reach out to me through Facebook Messenger (Facebook.com/theunicort)with any questions you have and I will do my best to offer you some helpful perspective.

When I asked my grandfather to write down his biggest piece of advice for me to live by on one of the last days of his life before his passing, he wrote to "listen first, then always act in the other's best interest, loving them with all your heart."

I want to do that for you.

- LOVE OTHERS MORE THAN SELF
- TREASURE YOUR RELATIONSHIPS
- VALUE FAMILY FIRST, ALWAYS

LISTEN FIRST, THEN ALWAYS ACT IN THE OTHERS BEST INTEREST, LOVING THEM WITH ALL YOUR HEART.

all my love
Grandp.
6/22/'10

Courtney Runyon is a motivational speaker, writer, and world traveler. As an autoimmune survivor, she has inspired hundreds of thousands of people through her social media to find the strength, gratitude, and faith necessary to overcome their own mental and physical roadblocks.

Courtney's story of recovery and renewal has been featured in major media outlets including The Daily Mirror and The Daily Star, and her appearance on Dallas' ABC TV station, WFAA Channel 8 News, won an Emmy in 2018.

She is currently traveling the world exploring different ways to heal, while organizing speaking gigs and women's retreats to share her method of alternative healing.

"Don't be afraid to speak your truth even if it isn't in alignment with popular opinion. Raise your voice in truth, honesty and compassion and experience the life you were meant to live."

Elizabeth Lupacchino, Cht, RMP

STORY 2

Shhh, Secrets, Don't Tell

Elizabeth Lupacchino

If I can just hold on one more day, one more hour, one more minute, one more second, I know I'll be OK. At least that's what I've heard. Maybe I'll close my eyes, and the pain will go away.

Prayer escapes me as God and His angels feel so far away. Somehow, I manage to hold on and keep pretending that everything is alright. After all, that's what I learned; put on a smile, pretend that nothing is wrong and keep going, so others don't know your pain. Who wants to be with someone who is mentally, physically, emotionally, or spiritually hurting.

I have been a very private person, and the hurt and trauma that I have endured have stayed hidden and made me the person I am today. I'm not bragging about what I have gone through, nor am I saying how I handled it was right.

Sure, there were many occasions that I would cry out, "Why me?"

Secrets, secrets, secrets; shh, don't tell! That's how I felt during this very bleak and dark time of my life. It was a time when the trust in a fellow human being was betrayed and created one of the darkest chapters in my life. Two young college students enjoying themselves to only have it end with my saying, "Why did this happen to me?" Shhh, secrets, don't tell.

Life goes on, we grow, we learn, we forgive, never quite forgetting. A few years later, I met someone who I believed in and trusted. We had so many things in common, same hobby, same friends, same religious beliefs, and family values. I was happy beyond words.

We had a storybook wedding surrounded by our family and friends only to have our marriage fall apart unexpectedly five years later. My husband was becoming a stranger. He would travel a lot and be gone days at a time.

This time was different. I was getting scared; I knew something wasn't right. My fears were validated on Labor Day weekend when I received a phone call. I heard a cheerful voice on the other end telling me that he was in California and was planning on staying there and not returning home.

I felt betrayed, belittled, deserted; crushed beyond words. I tried reaching out to friends and family for help and no one was around. Why would anyone be home? It was Labor Day weekend!

I felt the world crashing in on me and thought there was no way I could go on. One second, one minute, one hour; you can hold on! Shhh, secrets, don't tell. Don't do anything you will regret; he's not worth it!

How could I have been so blind as to not see that our commitment to each other was just a sham. It was then I made a promise to myself to never let a man hurt me that deeply again.

I still see that day in divorce court. My knees shook as I stepped down from the witness stand, and I tripped going back to my seat. I saw the sympathetic looks in the faces of the lawyers and the tears in my mother's eyes. I just kept going, kept believing, kept trusting that there had to be someone out there, someone who I could really trust and someone who would not take my trust and soulful commitment for granted.

Ten years went by and I met a man who said he loved me and wanted to be the father to our children. We dated, fell in love, got married, and that was when the nightmare began.

It wasn't long before this wonderful, gentle, caring man turned into someone I didn't know; someone I would grow to fear physically, mentally and emotionally. How could I have been so blinded? And again, I heard those words: hold on for one second, one minute, one hour, one day; you can do it.

This pain was new, it was sharp, it was profound. In one fell swoop, I lost my husband, my house. I went back on my promise to myself and did let a man hurt me that deeply. The trauma of the previous events came leaping at me and somehow, with my Angelic support and support of family and friends, I moved on.

The familiar, yet different, decree that once again I was single. I became immersed in my job, traveled with family and friends, joined choirs and choruses, and pursued new hobbies. I was alone but not lonely. The joy and love of singing led me to find a singing teacher and resume my lessons.

A friend told me of this incredible voice instructor. I went to one of his concerts and thought there is no way that I could take lessons from this man; he's too good! He is a singer, writer, composer, director. His other students are soloists who have gone on in their careers; one is even a famous opera singer. Why would he want to instruct me?

Three months later, I nervously, with sweaty hands and shaking voice, auditioned with him. I still remember his kind, soothing words, "This is the scariest thing you will ever have to do. It isn't about what your talents are or what you can do, but what I can do for you."

I worked hard and studied each and every week intently to prove to him, and to me, that I could do it. As each week went on, I felt something unfamiliar start to grow deep in my soul. It was like nothing I had ever experienced.

It was an emotion that I could not find words for. Was I falling in love with this man? How could it be; it's not how I have felt in the past. The feelings kept growing and kept me awake at night, wondering what I should do. If I tell him about my feelings, and if he isn't interested, I could lose him as an instructor. Or, he may still tell me he can't teach me any longer because of my feelings.

I was getting sick with worry of what to do. Shhh, secrets, don't tell! Finally, I decided to tell him how I felt. He was surprised and didn't take me seriously. As time elapsed, he realized that this was different. He was widowed and had no intention of ever remarrying.

I kept telling him to give us a chance. I knew it was the Divine bringing us together. All the suffering and betrayal of the past brought me to this point, to meet my heart of hearts. Someone who would accept me for all my flaws and ask me to be his wife. We keep pinching ourselves to make sure we're not dreaming.

Shhh, secrets, don't tell. Those words came back to me and I laughed; I laughed so loud. I don't have to keep a secret. I can trust once again. I let my guard down and trusted and believed in this gift from God. I didn't let the past get in the way of our beautiful future. We laugh, we cry, we enjoy being together and we tell each other our deepest secrets ... and it is OK! And yes, we are going to marry!

My clients relate to my life experiences: learning to trust, to let go, to believe in me, and our working together. You can heal from your past, your wounds.

I had a client who told me things about her childhood that were still affecting her life today. While she was still living at home, she started smoking. Her older siblings moved out, and her father started verbally abusing her, which made her smoke even more. Finally, she couldn't take it any longer and moved out to create a life of her own. It was not easy.

She went from a friend's house to another friend's house until she could finally make it on her own. She met a wonderful man who knew about her past and loved and accepted her as she was. When I met her, they were foster parents for a beautiful little girl and were going through the adoption process. She had quit her job so she could stay at home with her. She knew she had to quit smoking and was unable to do it on her own. She came to me, told me secrets, trusted me, believed in me, and asked me for my help. She wanted to quit smoking for her daughter, and most importantly for her own health so she could be there for her daughter.

We met weekly and pulled back the layers that were keeping her prisoner to the cigarettes. I helped her realize that they were her escape, her defiance against her father. She needed to go back to work and was going on several job interviews, but to no avail. She had to quit smoking and couldn't do it on her own.

We never gave up, and the week she completely stopped smoking, she got the perfect job that she hoped for. It was within walking distance to her house and within walking distance from the daycare. And, the judge unexpectedly awarded her and her husband custody of their little girl four months ahead of schedule and in time for

Christmas. Believe, trust, let go, and allow the magic of God, Spirit, Universe to be your guide, your Salvation, and bring you to where you need to be; however rocky the road may be.

You can learn more about Elizabeth on her website, ElizabethLupacchino.com, and she can be reached at elizlupacchino@aol.com. She is also extending a 10% discount and free initial consultation to all who mention this book.

Elizabeth Lupacchino, CHt, RMP, is a gifted healer with over 30 years' experience in helping woman achieve their mental, spiritual and emotional goals on this journey called life. As a certified Hypnotherapist, Past Life Facilitator, Master Reiki Practitioner and student of Shamanic Studies, Elizabeth has witnessed miracles in the people she has helped. Her workshops and seminars are very well attended and quickly sell out. As a speaker, Life Coach and published author, Elizabeth is able to reach and help people well beyond her geographical area.

"Live a life that would make a past version of you exclaim with wonder, 'Wow.' And, the version of the future would say, 'Thank you!!'"

Kristi Van Sickle

STORY 3

From Victim to Victor

Kristi Van Sickle

When you look in the mirror, what do you see? Do you see the face of a thriving woman who is confident? One who wakes up every day to accomplish her to-do list and work toward her dreams?

Or do you see a tired woman who feels stuck? A woman who has tried for too long and who feels defeated by life and, to be completely honest, is on the verge of giving up?

If the second description sounds more like you, pull up a chair. I understand.

I spent a couple of decades looking at that defeated woman in the mirror and doing nothing.

I'll be honest: deep down, I felt like I would never see a different reflection.

I was basically on a hamster wheel in life. Every day was the same. It was a "same song different verse" kind of existence. I felt like a failure. Useless. Hopeless. And sure, that I was definitely not enough.

My life was on a collision course with failure and disappointment. Survival seemed to be the only choice I had until it was all over — only to wake up and do it all over again.

At least, that's what I told myself.

You see, I spent years looking into the face of a woman who had fallen into a narcissist trap. And little by little, that relationship eroded my self-worth and replaced it with a perception that was anything but genuine. The problem is that I had been "trained" to believe it, and I was too blinded by the thoughts of everything I was NOT to be able to see everything that I am.

Trapped in a mental fog that overtook my thought processes, I had created my own version of a comfort zone that was anything but comfortable. I lived at a weight I hated. I was passing the years in a dead-end job. I convinced myself that I was basically broken and, therefore, undesirable and unlovable. I mean, who wants to be burdened by cleaning up a mess that's beyond hope?

So, there I stayed. Stuck in my own personal prison of misery, I lived my days convincing myself that it was easier to live in what I knew (even if it caused incredible pain) than to take a chance on what else might be out there.

Because what if I was a loser? What if I could not achieve anything worthy? What if I faced rejection? What if those miserable thoughts about just how "not enough" I am were actually true?

I didn't want to face the fear of discovering the truth. Because what if the reality hurt?

And then, one day, out of nowhere, I woke up to a new thought. So, what if the truth DID hurt? I mean, I was already hurting every day and had been for years. Could the "outside world" hurt me as much as I'd endured from people who claimed to love me? And even if it did, I had already proven my own strength. My own ability to survive in the danger zone. My own ability to overcome.

I had been pushed into a corner, and it was in that corner that I finally recognized my weariness and decided that I was tired of living a sham of a life.

I was tired of making allowances for the narcissist in my life and giving him the power to pen my story.

I was tired of allowing the controls of my life to be in the hands of someone else – especially knowing that, in doing so, I was sabotaging my own life.

The sun had broken through the murky clouds of my thoughts, and I was finally able to see clearly.

It was as though the lights had come on in an abandoned castle.... And when I looked around, I saw dusty old pieces of me that just needed to be noticed again. And nurtured. And put on display.

And it was time to do all that because, let's face it: we only get one chance at life! The days we're living are not a dress rehearsal. This is the live show! Your one and only chance at life.

I decided I wasn't going to live it behind the scenes, and I definitely wasn't going to live it playing a role I hated.

So, now what? (Cue the crickets.) I didn't know. It had been a long time since I had faced my days with hope.

I didn't even know how healthy couples were supposed to act. How love is supposed to look and feel.

I had to accept that I had been living on that rusty old hopeless hamster wheel, and I had to forgive myself for allowing it to last so long.

Then, I had to rediscover what normal looked like.

It had been so long that I honestly didn't have any idea where to start, but I was so determined to grab the steering wheel in my own life that I decided to research my options. Find people who could understand. People who had been there, done that, and could point me in the right direction.

My next step was to find a way to walk out on the life I knew. That would be hard because, for all the pain I had felt, there had been good times. Laughter. Shared jokes and memories. But under the surface of it always lived that pain that every victim of a narcissist knows too well.

Then, I knew I needed to explore my options and purposely design the life I wanted – and maybe more importantly, identify the life I DIDN'T want.

Once I knew those things, it was time to rebuild my life. One decision at a time.

One of the essential things I did was to resolve in my heart that I would no longer consider myself a victim. I would claim my rightful place as a survivor. Because I did it! I survived it, and I was going to live to not only tell about it but help other people out of it.

If you're in the same situation I was, please know that you, too, are a survivor. What should have crippled you ... made you give up ... crushed your spirit ... hasn't.

I've been where you are, and as scary as the unknown can be, I can promise you that the unknown can be more beautiful than you can imagine.

When you're stuck in what feels like the ruins of your life, it can be hard to remember what your dreams used to be or to believe in what life can be, but from the other side of the hopelessness, please know that you can still make your long-ago dreams of happiness a reality.

After many years, I can tell you that I've hung up the title of "survivor" of narcissistic abuse because I'm more than that. I'm a victor over it.

I'm blissfully married to the man of my dreams, and he and I often talk about how we have the "it" that everyone is looking for. It's just that so many people have given up on finding that they never reach the point of discovering what's out there for them.

I have a job I adore, and I'm blessed to be a mom to three of my favorite people in the world.

But all of that is not enough. I am also on a mission to help you find your hope. Your peace. Your happiness.

Trust me. I know it can be hard when you feel trapped in the darkness of a life you hate and find yourself with no light and direction. So, I want to help give that to you. I determined long ago that I would make my story matter and that I would find a way to point other women in the right direction.

And so, I've put together a four-part framework that will walk you through your healing process. Yes, each of the four steps has sub-steps, but you and I both know that making progress on any journey requires stopping points along the way.

Imagine you set out to make a cross-country journey. You would allow for restroom stops. Stops for meals. If the trip were long enough, you'd account for the need for overnight stops to shower and to recharge. Heck, you might even buy yourself some souvenirs along the way.

This is different only in that this journey is so much more than a vacation or a getaway. You are on a critical mission to save your own life. So, don't get bogged down with the thoughts of how long it's going to take or how many stops you may have to make.

Just dig down deep and find the courage to make the journey. It's worth it. How do I know that? Because I know you're worth it.

I'd love to welcome you into the healing space I've created on Facebook. It's called The Hope, Peace, and Happiness Hub, and it's full of women just like you who have decided to go from victim to survivor and are on the path to victory. (http://bit.ly/hphhkv)

Because I don't want you to leave your life and happiness up to chance, I am inviting you to a complimentary conversation with me for 30 minutes. We will come up with a strategy plan for you. You will be in charge if you want to continue our conversation or implement what you have learned from our session. YOU ARE IN CHARGE!!!

I'm on a mission to help you live a life you love. If you're ready for more out of life, reach out to me. I'm here to help.

Schedule your complimentary 30-minute Breakthrough Session at http://bit.ly/ConnectwithKristi.

Kristi Van Sickle is an accidental expert on narcissistic abuse. She is on a mission to put her years of real-life experience and diligent self-study to help other women start over after narcissistic abuse and create a life they love. Happily married and mother to her three favorite people in the world, Kristi is the author of *Unleashed: The Four-Part Framework to Help You Live a Limitless Life* and the creator of The Hope, Peace, and Happiness Hub. You can contact Kristi at Kristi@StartingOverStrategist.com, and be sure to subscribe to her newsletter and blog at www.StartingOverStrategist.com.

"You may walk the tightrope; however, what weighs on your mind is not determined by what is on the scale."

Janis Melillo

STORY 4

The Tightrope of Ghosting Yourself

Janis Melillo

I have always walked on that tightrope of my hopes, dreams and fears, yet somehow, I failed to see that I was drowning in that sea of despair and actually was ghosting myself. I could never seem to get my head above water so instead, I would indulge in all things "Chip" related.

Chips, chips and yes, more chips!! Chocolate chips, chocolate chip cookie dough, dark chocolate, mint chocolate chip ice cream, and please do not forget the infamous bag of potato chips; not the small bag nor those little lunch-size bags, oh no. We are talking about the family-sized bags of chips, you know, the size you would typically take to a picnic. Salted, vinegar potato chips - sure if you devour a bag of chips, then you have to balance it off with the sweet chips, which I listed above. Yes — I freely admit I have a huge "chip" problem — This chip problem goes way beyond an obsession — it was a cover-up to what was lurking beneath.

Having an obsession does not define who I am as a person, but it certainly led me to many moments when I was extremely unhealthy. So many people ask, then why would you proceed to consume something that is really an alternative to masking something a lot deeper? How do you get to that point where the impact of your actions adversely impacts your health to the point where you are tipping the scales at a very dangerous level?

I am not a clinical psychologist nor a therapist; therefore, my perspective and how I answer those questions come from a much more personal, deeper experience as related to what has or has not transpired in my life. For every action, there is a reaction, and my perception of events that have transpired are mine alone. I know that many of you reading my chapter will relate to this experience as something that you are going through in your life.

My moment of realization came in waves, but on one particular evening, as I followed my usual 9:30 p.m. routine, something drastic, in my opinion, happened. I would just get into bed and start to relax and watch a little TV when all of those fantastic food commercials would come on to the big screen TV — larger than life. Hmm, which chips would I choose? For some reason, the chocolate chip cookie dough at night always seemed to be my best option. I would literally get out of bed and contemplate opening the door of the refrigerator. The illuminating lights over the tub of chocolate chip cookie dough heightened my sense of gratification on what was to come. I literally could taste the thrill of the chips melting in my mouth. I would stand there for a moment and reflect - should I, or shouldn't I? Moreover, I chose to partake in this 9:30 p.m. "OCD" ritual — which stands for "Obsession Chip Draw."

I have OCD that bad that the desire and need I felt in that moment had happened all too often. Right then and there I had a choice. We all have choices; we can choose to do something we always do because it is normal and comfortable even though we know it is not necessarily good for us, or we can decide to make a decision to get healthy, go all in, which we also know may not be good for us; that is if we are unwilling to put in the work.

It's like we automatically set ourselves up for a natural disaster to happen before we even begin. Either way, if we are not in the right headspace, we need to make a rational, informed decision that will always lead us away from the wheel of tsunami self-destruction.

I loathed every single time putting myself in that tsunami wheel of self-destruction. Whichever decision I chose, I would emotionally beat myself up. You have to realize that at 9:30 p.m., it's challenging to have a rational, internal dialog with oneself because that overwhelming desire, the need to be in control in that exact moment to have what I wanted, what I wanted to do, and when exactly I wanted it, was such a magnet, a pull of force and energy — this was the type of addiction which went far beyond just food.

The food and my addiction to "chips" were more of an emotional roller coaster of what could have been. In order to move forward and get healthy, I had to be totally honest with myself and unapologetically put myself first. For many women, including myself, this is not how we operate, so why is putting ourselves first so difficult? For some, this may be easy, but I felt a whole slew of emotions all at once. I was emotionally spent tipping the scales at 262 lbs. — the shame and criticism I felt as a plus-size female was disheartening.

How the heck did I get so unhealthy, which only seemed to me to be a short amount of time? How was I going to move forward feeling criticism from other people (and from myself as well); feeling the rejection that perhaps caused me to even body shame myself?

This was not okay; to body shame oneself is to self-destruct without a parachute; such an unhealthy state of mind — that freakin' circle of self-loathing, not feeling worthy, wheel of self-destruction was rearing its' ugly head. I think I was at that point where I really needed to be totally honest with myself; be real; be accepting and, first and foremost, be gentle and kind to myself. This was a true test and reflection of the Mirror to My Soul.

The reflection in the mirror on this particular day was almost daunting. I paused for a moment, which seemed like an eternity of jumbled, mixed emotions. Good, bad, or indifferent, I realized that in solitude, I would outwardly speak to myself and carry on quite a conversation. Although at times, this often makes me giggle, I realized the gravity and seriousness of the turmoil I put my health through and how my emotions were directing my eating frenzy to feed my addiction. I had to look at food differently and not go on another diet! I wanted to nurture my body with healthy food that fed my soul and nourished my body; not go for the temporary fix, which would mask my problems.

I knew it was time to get serious, knowing that the road ahead to get to my ultimate destination would take me to places unknown, yet would, in the end, make me appreciate the journey to health that much more. Where do I go to do this? How do I do this? So many questions, yet my answers, were unknown. I knew this: was my hard work going to be worth it — heck yes!!

My destination was finally reached, not without a lot of muscle pain, not without a lot of self-discovery, but with a healthy dose of "wow, I did it!" I obtained what I thought was impossible (I lost about 122 lbs.). I felt such a sense of responsibility, so powerful and so fulfilling that I had to share what I learned about this incredible healthy journey.

The impact of my weight loss was not only felt by me, but also those around me. It was in that moment that I knew I wanted to spark that interest in others as well. I became a health coach, having completed my studies with the Institute for Integrative Nutrition. It is my mission, my passion for helping others achieve what they think may be impossible.

As simple as it may sound, as a result of

implementing positive changes, we create a sense of self-worth, and our value is determined by not what the number is on the scale but the journey we took to get to where we want to be — a much healthier version of ourselves!

As an experienced health coach, I collaborate with my clients — it's a true partnership. I don't advise; in other words, I don't put my clients on a "diet." Personally, I don't believe in diets (that's a topic for another book!). I lead them to discover and unearth their true potential. Creating, rebuilding the belief in themselves, allows my clients to believe and see who they truly are — a much healthier version of themselves!

A journey such as this does not require "willpower." It requires the ability to change a few small things at a time. This starts on Day #1 when we start working with one another. We often reflect on the weight of their emotions rather than the weight that shows up on the scale. We establish and create goals together; I don't give advice. I coach my clients on where they want to go and how they can get there.

At some point in their journey, we will have a conversation about "movement." Movement is the exercise that a lot of us have forgotten about. (By the way, you don't have to join the gym — true story!)

When my clients expand their capacity to achieve their desired goals, that is what it is all about, and that is why in many respects, I am so grateful that my tightrope of ghosting myself has inspired me to help others!

Janis Melillo is an Amazon #1 International Best-Selling Author having co-authored 13 books to date. She is a health coach and shares her unlimited passion for wellness through nutrition and fitness. Janis is a firm believer that every client she coaches does NOT go on a diet but rather cultivates small changes to adhere to a healthy lifestyle change. Along with her love of health coaching, she is an avid proponent of adding value to people's lives. She is the author of many inspirational and motivational books. Janis has also been the featured speaker at different women's events and organizations.

To schedule your free 1-hour health coaching session with Janis, please contact her at: (386) 717-0914 or email: Janis.Weighs2HealthLLC@gmail.com.

"Your attitude determines your response to difficult challenges that come your way, not the challenge."

Sherry Wurgler

STORY 5

The Leader in You

Sherry Wurgler

Sitting in a coffee shop — here comes Jenna wearing the biggest smile, her purse bouncing at her shoulder in time with her step. She has the look of someone who is on top of the world. She sits down across from me and before even saying "Hi," the words spill out, "I got the promotion!" The look on her face says everything, pure joy, and expectation. She can't contain herself in telling me just what this means to her. Jenna spends the next few minutes telling me about the interview, the wait, and now, just today, the news that she was chosen for the position she has been longing for.

Stirring our lattes, Jenna takes me back to the first time we met, to the first time we started talking about the journey to become a leader. She shared with me what it meant to be mentored and how it helped her emerge into the confident woman she was today.

"Do you remember all the fears I had. I can remember the first day I stepped foot on the unit. I didn't want to be noticed. I tried to hide, disappear into the woodwork. Scared to death that someone would ask me something I didn't know. Scared to death, I couldn't say the right answer. Scared to death that I would forget everything I had been taught in class. Scared to death, I couldn't fulfill the expectations of my role. Even though I was new, the job stretched my learning curve to a new and more profound level, a level, even as a beginner, I didn't know if I was prepared. What if I made a mistake? What would my peers think of me? What would my supervisor feel about me? My insecurities threatened to overtake me and consume me with doubt and uncertainty. I was scared to trust myself. Afraid to speak up. Hesitant to have an opinion. Did my opinion actually count? Of course, how would anyone know of my opinion, I barely speak up! And then you came over to me and said something I will never forget, 'If you need help, just ask. There are no silly or stupid questions. We've all been where you are! So, speak up when you need help; I don't bite! We will do things together, and gradually you will learn to have confidence and trust your own intuition and knowledge. I'll walk with you and be your guide. You'll get there, don't worry!"

Jenna proclaimed how strengthening and encouraging those words were for her to hear! It made my heart swell. My passion is to help others become the leader of their own life, and in turn, become a leader who mentors others in the same way.

Jenna continued in her reverie.

"I was able to express my ignorance, lack of confidence, doubt, insecurities, and you just replied by tackling one of those fears, accomplishing that goal to a positive resolve, and more or less, checking those fears and doubts off my list. It was feeling free to discuss difficult situations that made the difference in feeling sure of myself and developing more and more trust and security in coming to my own solutions."

Yes, there were times you offered another solution to the problem that was better, more efficient, and effective than mine, and a time or two, vice versa. What really had a positive influence was when you recognized my efforts to come up with a workable solution that hadn't been tried before. You didn't need to do things as they have always been done; you encouraged creative and innovative brainstorming, thinking outside the box.

Everyone wants to believe they are able to enact change that will help ease or improve time management and workflow, whether it may be at a personal level or business/profession level. Giving those ideas air and space to grow into fruition is one of the attributes of a leader. Getting lost in "the way it's always been done" puts a damper on the creative process and holds businesses in a stagnant position that keeps them from moving into the next generation of growth and development.

I see the sparkle and enthusiasm in Jenna's expression and realize how much she has embraced and personalized her style of leadership. She has grown her own wings! She has confidence, assertiveness, and handles herself with grace and respect. She is learning continuously to stay on the cutting edge as she is recognized as a leader in her own right. Those qualities will take her far in communicating with others in the business world, and also the personal/private realm. She has set her course and that course looks rich with promising outcomes! She goes on to describe in detail how our interactions helped her grow in confidence, self-assurance, and assertiveness.

We started with the basics. Clarity of purpose. What was our goal, purpose, and what would the results look like? What would the professional outcomes look like, and what would the personal accomplishments look like. What would the all-around gains be in the end? As Stephen Covey says, "begin with the end in mind." Confidence enhances the path to success. Believe you can achieve it, and you are halfway there! Trust supports confidence and self-esteem. So, where does trust stem from? Within. Everything we need is found within ourselves. When we feed ourselves the proper emotional fuel, we not only survive the difficulties in life; we THRIVE!

And let's face it! Businesses have their ups and downs, rough spots, and just when you think you have everything figured out, something comes along to shake things up and cause doubt and confusion! How you deal with those tough times either increases your resilience or depletes it! I worked with Jenna on increasing her resilience to get through any circumstance that came her way, the difficult - the stressful - and the seemingly impossible! Jenna and I started by creating a positive mindset. Positive in, positive out. Positive thoughts help increase self-confidence and self-esteem, the building blocks of personal development, step one on the road to personal and professional leadership. The first step in leadership development is developing a positive mindset. As Brian Tracy says, "You are what you think you are!" Mindset is everything! So let's discuss the benefits of positive mentality.

Successful people adhere to a positive mindset that will set them toward futuristic ideas, solution-oriented and problem solving. Successful people don't lose themselves in negative and demeaning beliefs, attitudes, and lifestyles. Professionals that are on track with their goals have an upbeat and resilient mentality that attracts other like-minded people, i.e., successful people. And that, my friend, is what you want to emulate.

Success breeds success. A positive mentality aligns with one's core beliefs.

I talked with Jenna about her goals, how she expected to attain those goals, and we worked on a plan to achieve those same goals! Positive mindset was step one on her path to accomplishing her expectations and goals. We talked about setting her thoughts on the right track first thing in the morning. The positive affirmations that would lead to a positive outlook and approach for her upcoming shift. Next, we talked about the self-limiting beliefs that hold us back from attaining our true potential.

I talked with Jenna about the setbacks that could come up during work. The unforeseen emergent situations that needed an on the spot identification and resolve. We discussed the resources she had at her fingertips and a step away. The closest and best resources - her peers- just a step away. Experience speaks volumes, and her peers can offer her their history of past experiences and give constructive advice on the most effective and efficient answer. Thinking fast on her feet would be something Jenna would grow into quickly by applying her newfound knowledge combined with the lessons already learned by her peers. Doubt and uncertainty follow "new" staff when they first step into their profession. But, if met with confidence, enthusiasm, and a positive mindset from her peers, this newbie will soon learn the ropes and become an excellent fit for the professional culture.

Jenna expressed her concerns about making a mistake or not being efficient in accomplishing a task. We talked about working together on those more involved tasks and then reviewing those steps later in a more relaxed setting. She feared not keeping up, and we discussed prioritizing needs and time management. We talked of letting go of the doubt and critical condemnation that often comes when one starts a new venture. Self-limiting beliefs would just keep Jenna feeling small and useless when her spirit was enthusiastic for learning. The truth is, we are far more competent and capable then we can ever imagine.

I did little talking, sitting across from Jenna and letting her revel in her newfound confidence and excitement over her job. I just listened to her expound on how she handled a difficult situation and felt in command and sure of her decisions. Her insight was growing into the maturity and depth of a well-seasoned professional.

Had it only been a year since I first met her, soon after graduation? Walking so close behind me the first day, I nearly tripped over her when I turned around. She has come into her own, and that was a beautiful sight.

Do you find yourself in Jenna's position? Are you feeling overwhelmed and unsure of yourself? Do you have trouble reaching your goals because of self-limiting beliefs and negative mindset? I am a *Transformational Leadership Coach* and will help you navigate those feelings and experiences to a positive end. Let's connect on Facebook, and let's talk about your future pursuits and goals.

Sherry Wurgler is a mother of 4 amazing children and a grandmother to 5 wonderful grandchildren that are near and dear to her heart. She is a practicing RN working in the field of psychiatry. She is also a Transformational Leadership Coach. During her life's journey, she has worked with women empowering women to become the leaders of their own lives. Her memoir, "Surviving Ritual Abuse," received #1 best seller on Amazon. She has also co-authored several other international bestsellers. Tough times are best met with a resilient spirit. As she expands her coaching presence, she is ready to help women soar through life's adversities with courage and resilience. Connect with her on Facebook, Facebook messenger, or at www.sherrywurgler.com.

"Get giddy painting what you envision and want in your life. We only have today, this very moment. And each one is a present waiting for you not only to see it; EMBRACE IT!"

Toni Jo Beck

STORY 6

Embracing Vision

Toni Jo Beck

After surviving childhood trauma, betrayal, and divorce, I never imagined a small drive would cause me to contemplate jumping off the 6th-floor balcony of my hotel room. Yet after a car accident injured my eye and made the very act of seeing painful, that is precisely where I found myself. My head hurt so bad, and I was feeling suffocated not being able to take care of myself, let alone the pressure of being solely responsible for my four children. There is no doubt in my mind that we are all capable of creating miracles on this earth, and I prayed fervently to my Heavenly Father to help me find mine at that moment.

Although it took longer than I would have preferred to receive all the blessings of my miracle, what I learned on this journey has transformed my life and has given me a mission to help others do the same.

After a forced nap, while sitting in that hotel room, I knew I could not make excuses. It was my choice, and I was determined to recover. I had to focus more on taking care of myself and committed right then and there that I was going to do whatever it took to get better and heal myself. As a mom, this was harder than it may seem as I was used to giving a lot of attention to my children, and the road to my recovery was difficult and very time-consuming. My brain was working so hard to put together the images in my world at times that everything else would shut down. In those moments, I could see people's mouths moving but not understand what they were saying nor even hear their words as they were talking to me. I would fall asleep often when I would sit down and not be able to wake up. Seeing was painful, nauseating, and no longer reliable, and this new reality was hard to accept. Everything I now struggled with, even simple tasks that used to be so easy. The complexity of it all hit me after my accident when I could not read the street sign clearly and worsened when emergency responders asked me the names of the passengers in our vehicle that was now totaled. I started bawling as I told them I could not remember my own children's names.

At first, I did not understand the magnitude of my situation, thinking I just had a concussion that affected my sight and memory. I planned on resting and feeling back to normal after a couple of weeks. Although, as that period passed, it was not improving, and my Vision was only getting worse. Going against the advice of medical doctors who kept telling me to be patient and that I needed more time to recover, I made an appointment with an eye specialist. They found that my retina was actively detaching, and I was sent in for emergency laser surgery to get it repaired. Again I thought it would take a few weeks, and then I would feel back to normal. As that time came and went, my life was nowhere close to the normal I had been used to. Continually I searched out treatments and resources to help myself recover. The one thing that I stuck to through numerous months of therapies and treatments was my determination to restore my Vision.

My journey to recovery started with letting go in so many ways. Starting with all of the physical stuff we no longer needed and clearing the visual clutter in my environment. Simplifying and getting rid of anything that was not fundamental was very freeing. Releasing the expectations of what I should be doing each day and not getting frustrated with myself for no longer being able to do what I had been able to do. It was learning to be okay with right where I was and my current situation. Even having to let go of the things I excelled at, that were no longer serving me. It was simplifying my life and getting back to the basics. It was multi-layered and messy at times, and as I went deeper into this process, it involved releasing the emotions and anger I had been holding onto and had allowed to bind me in ways that were only holding me back. Letting go of expectations allowed me to be able to see and appreciate what I had. For example, one of the many things that colored my life, I did not want to get divorced.

    I was stuck in the victimhood of someone else's decision that affected not having my family look as I had planned. In releasing that expectation, I began to see what I had with an eye of gratitude and excitement for the beautiful family in front of me. That crisis is a catalyst for change as it narrows the focus, and if we allow it, it opens our hearts and paves the way for infinitely more. Our ability to see is so complex and so magnificent, and every day prior, I had taken that for granted. Learning that all of us have a blind spot in our field of Vision. That we see colors through separate areas of sight, and the sequences of those fields affect the way we see the world and so much more. The ability to slow down and appreciate the present moment is truly a gift that should not be overlooked. I have felt my heart continually expand the deeper I dare to dive into this process of letting go and releasing the weight of all that was holding me back from really seeing what I had before and living in the joy of each moment.

My journey progressed with a discovery at a follow-up appointment, testing my balance. I had to stand on one leg and not fall over. With my eyes open, I had minor problems balancing on one leg, but as soon as I closed my eyes, I twisted and jerked involuntarily. Contemplating this as I wondered why it was so tricky, I mentally chose to drop down into my heart. I knew I could do this, and the floor was not moving underneath my foot, so I took a deep breath and trusted completely on that knowledge envisioning in my mind the room around me, and instantly I had found my stability again. That moment was so exciting for me and was the start of my journey of finding clarity in my Vision with my eyes closed. It started with envisioning my surroundings with my eyes closed, which helped me to increase my actual field of view and showed me the opportunity to create what I wanted in my life. That my Vision is only a picture created through the lens of my perceptions, and injury, emotionally and physically, can both affect the lenses through which we see our understanding perception of that reality. I began to heal my sight by seeing more clearly with my eyes closed. I could envision what was in front of me and create the image through my eyes. Learning to let go of how I wanted it to be and appreciating what was, playing within the realms of my new reality. The stability I found while trying to balance on one foot, I found in relationships that were struggling. The pain of past grievances can make us unstable in the way we react with those we love. By diving into my heart, releasing the fear and hurts I had wanted to cling to at times as justification for my behaviors that were not in alignment with who I am inside, I found the nature of my relationships I valued improving. It was focusing on what was fundamentally important to creating the desired outcome I want in my life. Then trusting what I knew to be true in every fiber of my being while envisioning what I knew was possible. I started creating my reality as I continued the process of letting go of what was not in alignment with that Vision.

Discovering that my heart is smarter than my brain and allowing myself to operate from my heart. Our brains are like computers, and if there is a processing error, it slows down and does not always give us clear signals of benefit for our use. And most importantly, I learned that by dropping into my heart, the source of intuition and love, I could bypass the mental instability and create a firm foundation from which to operate. Trusting myself. It created a firm foundation from which to live my life. At times I suffer from overthinking each situation and find myself stuck in analysis paralysis. Causing tremendous heartache, grief, and loss when I doubted myself or resisted what I knew instead of committing to and leaning into my heart's power. Hanging on to what I think or need and not being willing to let things go, prevents us from progressing forward. When we open our hearts to our present moment and learn to appreciate all that it entails, even when it's hard and painful, we receive countless more blessings and opportunities that we would have talked ourselves out of otherwise. Taking the time to stop and envision the desired outcome and then going forward with complete faith to create it. Not allowing ourselves to get stuck in the endless list of what needs to be done or sucked into the entertainment barrage designed to distract us from the very things that bring us love and joy. Letting go of what is not necessary, and freeing myself to paint my reality on the mural of each day. Bringing excitement, love, and joy to bask in the rays of its warmth. I am grateful for my journey and would not give up the knowledge I gained by going through this experience.

It took learning to see with my eyes closed. Fighting to regain my Vision because I decided that staying where I was, was not an option! And that was my solution. Dropping in my heart and committing to an outcome. Falling in my heart with trust in myself, restored my inner Vision, and began my path to get clarity and stability in my life. Focusing on faith in the things that really mattered to me. Then using my challenges as a catalyst to focus my Vision, I choose to see joy, love, and gratitude with every sunrise and sunset. If you want to stay married, don't complain about how horrible your spouse is. If you want your kids to grow to be successful and feel loved, you can't yell at them when things don't go your way - or belittle them each time they don't meet your expectations.

Get back into your heart. Choose to love and include yourself in that equation! Yes, you. Love yourself! Right, where you are, don't wait for the house or the new job or the perfect spouse or whatever else you think will bring you momentary happiness. The ability to slow down and appreciate this present moment is truly a gift; it is my miracle delivered, that you should not overlook. Choose NOW! Now is your moment and choose to find EVERYTHING in that space there is to love. Even a painful experience that is helping you grow and develop into a better version of yourself. Stop reacting to what occurs or doesn't each day and get giddy painting what you envision and want in your life. We only have today, this very moment. And each one is a present waiting for you not only to see it; EMBRACE IT!

Please visit www.embracingvision.com/freegift for a free gift to help you on your way to finding your Vision!

Toni Jo Beck is an avid adventurer of all things in life. Born in Utah and raised in Washington, she looks forward to being at the beach. She loves to spend time outdoors, reading, exploring, and traveling with her children. She is a natural public speaker, author, and motivator who helps expand the hearts and visions of her audience. She offers coaching and courses to help her clients find clarity in their Vision and unlock their divine potential. Tune in to her top-ranked podcast show, "Embracing Vision" weekly.

*"Reveal the masterpiece within you.
The time to take action is now!"*

Divya Parekh

STORY 7

Living The Life You Want

Divya Parekh

On a beautiful August Tuesday evening, when we were walking towards our hotel after having a sumptuous meal, the clouds broke open. The darkness descended upon us quickly, and we could barely see each other in the pouring rain. One minute, I was giggling as the rain pounded on us. The next, I heard a bloodcurdling scream, and everything went blank.

As I regained consciousness, I was tasting the concrete. All I could feel was the searing pain on my right side. My family pulled me up slowly. We entered the hotel lobby and asked the receptionist for the nearest hospital. She shared that the nearest one was 25 miles away. I cursed myself for picking one of the remotest areas in South Dakota. Being an optimist, I thought stopping here would be no problem before getting on a 12-hour flight the next day. Sitting at the airport, my right arm in a makeshift sling, I got a doctor's appointment on Friday because nothing was available on Thursday.

I was joking with the X-ray technician that it was probably nothing. She raised her eyebrows and gently tried to straighten out my right arm. I heard that doggone bloodcurdling scream again. You guessed correctly — it was me. They sent me off to the big dogs — to a CAT scan and an MRI. I found out that my right shoulder broke in multiple places. Instead of sympathy from the family, doctor, and nurses, they dished out glaring looks aimed at me for delaying the medical visit.

Because of the way the bone breaks were, surgery was not an option. My shoulder took a long time to heal, resulting in complications. During this time, I often crowned myself, "The Poor Me Grumpy Queen." My world had diminished to a small area of existence, with only a few resources within my reach. Since my ability to move without excruciating pain was so profound, I set up a recliner in my living room. I sat there by day and slept (or tried to) by night. I could no longer drive, write, type, prepare food, shower, change clothes, or get up from that darned chair without help. I was experiencing life as an invalid, something that I didn't think would happen until old age — if at all. I felt distressed because not only was I physically in pain, but I was also dealing with mental, emotional, and financial burdens to carry on my one good shoulder. As if I did not have enough on my plate, my medical plan had high deductibles. I thought my business was going to shatter into little pieces like glass as my medical debt piled over $35,000 for two years. I didn't know if my business or I would ever be the same again. I felt foreign to myself and often wondered, "Who is this alien creature I have turned into?" All was gloom and doom!

Then, one day, I was fortunate to fall into deep meditation after taking pain medication. I realized that I was miserable about being miserable. I made a split-second decision to create a shift. Subsequently, having learned to handle my swinging emotions, I learned to live by the phrases, "Necessity is the mother of invention," "I am okay to be human," and "Perfection is the roadblock to progress." During my reflective, positive waves, I began to garner my mind, emotions, and actions for the arduous journey of recovery. I often thought of my "Why." I reminded myself that my "why" is about my love of people and connections. I began to allow myself to be vulnerable, to put my pride on the back burner, and to ask for help.

Surprisingly, the relationship bonds with my closest friends and colleagues became very robust. The more I asked for help, the more people offered. It was a very eye-opening concept that I began to explore in-depth. I wondered what made these great people so willing to help me, even beyond what I asked.

At first, I had a misconception that my injury stole a year and a half out of my life. I later realized that it provided me with the equivalent of years of learning, growing, and gaining momentum in a relatively short period. I learned a perspective that I could be a flawed human who could support others while receiving help. I encouraged my relationships by listening to their woes and challenges, as well as helping them in their personal and professional growth. What I thought might be the death knell for my business became a wave of creativity and ingenuity that kept my business alive. I was also able to keep somewhat of a routine personal and home life with the help of friends and family.

As the end of the year following my adventure approached, I spent some time in reflection, and I was pleasantly surprised that I kept my sanity through it all. I stayed true to my "Why." I had a massive personal evolution making my soul richer in so many ways. I am happy to say that I was able to pay off my debt and take my business to the next level! Now, I am hungry and focused on making a MASSIVE IMPACT on MILLIONS! The lifeblood of my business are people and relationships. Let's look at the relationships that have moved the dial for me and my clients.

Relationships

The substance of everything I teach is that you need to focus on your vision of what you want and that you mindfully develop relationships of significance with yourself and others to achieve it. You might underestimate the power you have to design your life. You might feel stuck in your personal or professional life. I have discovered through my own experience, and by helping others learn to develop the types of relationships I have, that you can achieve professional and personal fulfillment at the same time. These connections allow us to bring more joy, more love, and more freedom to our lives.

A word here on mindfulness. As a definition, mindfulness is a conscious choice of living in the present, guided by value-based decisions and non-judgments. Mindfulness is also living with grace. As we focus on our goals, grace weaves its way into day-to-day activities and relationships.

Mindfulness brings self-awareness without

judgment. Knowing yourself is the foundation of authenticity. Non-judgment allows you to be accepting of your strengths and limitations. You are open to finding out about your blind spots and emotional hindrances. You can turn them into assets, driven by the values and support of friends and mentors. Mindfulness makes you want to grow and allows you to learn from your life experiences — failures and successes alike — while retaining humility.

It is necessary to exercise mindfulness as you explore the relationships you have with yourself and others. Some relationships may be more natural; others might take more effort. Regardless, the more you concentrate and work on a relationship, the easier it will be to integrate into your life. In this chapter, we will explore the nine essential relationships (self, time, money, market, team, partners, death, results, and legacy) that when illuminated in our consciousness, when embraced with grace and mindfulness, give us access to the humility and the potential for resilient altruism that is a prerequisite for sharing oneself with others. These serve as the foundational bedrock for developing relationships and connections with others.

Relationship with Self

You might be saying, "I understand that you need to have relationships with various people to have success in your life's work, but what do you mean a relationship with yourself?" We do need relationships to do what we want in life. First, we need to have a clear understanding of ourselves before we can do anything. You must be clear on the values and message you share with yourself and others. With clarity, you will be empowered and prepare yourself for the desired outcome. Developing this relationship with self empowers you to speak out and communicate authentically. It is the crucial stepping-stone to developing superb leadership skills.

Relationship with self is the underpinning of your life's joy, freedom, and success. When you let core values and mindfulness be your guiding compass, you:

- Will be able to stand up for yourself without being a doormat.
- Will be able to forgive others for your sake and take the lessons learned from experiences to grow yourself and others.
- Will increase your self-trust, self-confidence, and achieve peak performance.
- Will, on the whole, build a rock-solid

foundation that will weather both good and challenging times with equanimity.

Relationship with Time

One of my coaching clients, Lina, had a misguided relationship with time. She mistook busy for being productive. She couldn't understand how she could work 12 hours a day and not seem to get anywhere. She had started her own software company and was frustrated at the inequity between her daily activity and profits.

As we worked together, Lina realized that time is the most valuable currency of life. The key to understanding a relationship with time is knowing where you are in your life right now, and where your personal and professional life is going to be in the long term. Once Lina's vision for her life became clear, she was able to use her time wisely by minimizing distractions, and taking the RIGHT actions. Her company began to thrive, and she had more free time to enjoy the fruits of her labor.

Relationship with Money

People can have a complicated relationship with money. It is crucial to think about what your relationship with money is, especially when you want to increase your profits substantially. It's great to earn it, but it is better to understand early on how to discipline yourself in its use. What you do with your money is the most critical component of your relationship with it.

Nothing illustrates more of a person's nature than what they do with money, particularly when they have either an extreme abundance or scarcity of it. When you align vision and values with personal and professional life, you can achieve balance. This connection carries over to money.

Your money mindset allows you to know what having money means and that money is not evil. It gives you the freedom to be mindfully aware of the present moment while knowing that your decisions and actions determine the results.

Your money mindset is going to determine the league you play in. If you think small, you are going to work with clients who want to play in a minor league, or take opportunities that keep you in your comfort zone. If you believe that there is no limit to your business growth, your efforts will focus on clients who want you to help them grow to the next level. You will also seek out opportunities that will catapult you to unimagined levels. When you bring all your values into your work, your business will grow exponentially.

Relationship with Market

The relationship with money motivated me to understand my market. Knowing your market is essential whether you have your own business, or are an executive in a large corporation. We all have a market depending on our business niche. Relationship with the market is knowing and understanding your ideal client, establishing your brand, making a positive impact, and serving your clients to help them succeed in their personal, professional, and financial goals. By aligning yourself with your market, you can provide the best solutions for your clients in your area of expertise.

I have had more than one client who felt like they were spinning their wheels trying to grow their business. Many times, the solution was to help them realize their company did not know or understand their customers well. I helped them build a loyal customer base by shifting their shotgun approach of trying to be everything to everybody to one of connecting and forming relationships with those who could benefit the most from their products or services.

Relationship with Team

When you work with people to achieve a common goal, a healthy relationship with your team is essential. Within a team, the leader is the catalyst that drives his or her team to thrive, so each member provides extreme value both individually and collectively. If you are the leader of a team, you are responsible for strengthening the relationship among the team members.

When I work with organizational or business teams, I help them become high performing teams with humanistic values. The focus is on purpose, encouragement, real-time feedback, and reinforcing structures. Happy team members play a significant role in each other's personal, professional, and financial success because they help accomplish the team's and the company's goals. When you work as a collaborative team, everybody is involved in planning, designing, developing, and implementing those goals. When you achieve the goals, the entire team cheers and celebrates. After all, they helped make it happen!

When you have a connected team, the contributions and support enable you to orchestrate productivity, innovation, creativity, and the best quality products and services. This profitability enhances everyone's life.

Relationship with Partners

Business is a system in which all parts and processes contribute to the success or failure of the whole. We all work with other professionals outside of our organization or business. These specialists or contractors help us with various aspects of our company. You might want partners who share in every aspect of your company from the initial establishment to sustainable success, or the purpose may be to work together for one particular project. The partner could be someone who specializes in a different industry than yours, but his or her company complements yours perfectly because they bring a different perspective to business operations. By joining forces, you grow together.

Whatever your intention is with a partner, it is important to realize that it is about collaborating, not competing. You are pooling resources of the mind and heart. With your partner, you want to create more opportunities, create more emotional and financial wealth, and go beyond what you can do alone. It also means that you sometimes need to have difficult conversations if you have people who are not keeping up their end of the bargain.

For example, I formed a partnership with a book publisher, and we put together a written contract. The contract defined clear expectations including roles and responsibilities of both parties. However, the publisher failed to deliver their end of the agreement. After several unsuccessful attempts to salvage the relationship, I decided to cut them loose. Sometimes, working on a relationship with a partner involves limiting your losses before things become irreparable.

Relationship with Death

As they say, nothing is certain except death and taxes. Our 21st century society tries to insulate us from death. However, proximity to death or failure forces us to explore our fears and feelings about the subject. Doing so gives us the opportunity to live our lives in a new and fulfilling manner.

This relationship is about accepting fear, working through it, and using the grit that you have deep inside of you to overcome it. It is about living life rather than passing through it.

Shakespeare said, 'A coward dies a thousand times before his death, but the valiant taste of death but once.' By establishing your relationship with death, you learn to live with that fear in your life. It will help you overcome challenges, go after new opportunities, and set your affairs to take care of your loved ones and your business in the event of your death.

Relationship with Results

Your connection with results matters! Results are the milestones that tell us if we're going in the right direction. Success requires destination and destination need direction. Life is a journey comprised of many goals. It is about living a mindful life driven by value-based decisions, learning, unlearning, and relearning while having fun. The relationship with results is how you measure success, clearly defining outcomes, determining progress, and learning from failures as you work toward your goals.

This relationship can take on many forms. I have worked with people who did not know how to handle their success. They didn't know what to do with it, how to continue it, or how to leverage it into significant positive results. Think of that as you get closer to achieving your goals. Are you going to know what to do once you get there?

I had issues with my results when starting in my coaching career. I was working with great clients and having a degree of success regarding activity and income, but I wasn't happy with it.

I evaluated my business growth and mindfully applied the lessons learned from successes and failures. This helped me scale up my business. I went from coaching individual clients to coaching teams and departments in bigger companies. Being comfortable in the relationship with my results allowed me to speak to several hundred people at once and write books to help many others.

Relationship with Legacy

Finally, there is the relationship with legacy. Usually, when we think of a legacy, it is what we leave behind after we leave this world. We all like to believe others will remember us because of what we will leave behind. This is true to an extent, but you can start your legacy NOW!

Empowerment has a ripple effect. Your fiery message can ignite a passion in someone else.

Every time you act as a leader with your message, you enable others to choose challenges with courage.

There is so much you can do today that will leave an impression on someone's future. It might be working with kids or seniors or animals. It can be working with a local nonprofit or being on the board of a national organization. You never know when giving of yourself is going to impact a person's future. You might not even know them personally, but your efforts could change someone's life forever.

My Legacy

Part of what I teach others and advocate in my own life is creating a sustained solution. I donate a portion of my books' profits to KIVA (Kiva.org). It is an international nonprofit connecting people through lending to alleviate poverty. By giving as little as $25 to Kiva, anyone can help a borrower start or grow a business, go to school, access clean energy, or realize their potential.

For some, it's a matter of survival; for others, it's the fuel for a life-long ambition.

I take a great interest in the lives of our youth. I do not look at it as a cliché but as truth: Children are our future. In some places, our youth have limited access to educational opportunities that could shape their lives and community for the better. I prefer to partner with organizations that take a systematic approach to address root issues rather than slap a Band-Aid on a problem. So, I partner with TMT Youth Community Foundation, a nonprofit organization that focuses on accessing, developing, and growing the talents of young people. I also partner with The Little Maker's Academy that focuses on collaborative learning and critical thinking with young students through hands-on STEAM activities.

I also work with Inspire NC, a student-led non-profit organization whose aim is to promote interest, knowledge, and involvement in the fields of STEAM and develop leadership in the next generation. Through Inspire NC, I mentor a Robotics Team. These young people build and operate robots. They have fun doing it… I don't know how many of them will become great scientists or engineers in the future, but I know what I do is having an impact on their lives.

My work with relationships is one of my legacies, and I take seriously the contribution I make to others' lives. I believe that when you make a difference in your life, a loved one's life, or someone else's, one blend into another. When you are confident in your passion, you work at it. I have a passion for making a difference. I want to reach out and genuinely help others. I find opportunities to do that every day, whether it is something small or a larger endeavor. Let today become the springboard for empowering love in your and others' lives every day.

Live the Life You Want

Grateful I am,
For who I am.
Today, I am,
Ready to take on tomorrow.
When I look back on today,
I have no sorrow.
Right or wrong, choices I will make,
Every day, for my sake
Action over inaction
Purpose, pain, and passion
Learning to unlearn and relearn
Prepared for what awaits me,
Around every corner, I turn.
Support each other,
And grow together.
Build relations
And bridge nations.
Live your legacy.
There's no fallacy.
Achieving success, happier than ever.
Reducing our stress in this joyful endeavor.
The future is now our present.
Nimbly unwrap your return on investment.

Will You Leave a Book Review?

Did you enjoy this book and find it useful?

We will be very grateful when you post a short review and give your success story on Amazon right now!

Your support makes a difference. We read and respond to all the reviews personally to make this book even better!

To leave a review right now, go to www.amazon.com.

ABOUT THE ART OF UNLEARNING FOUNDERS

Divya Parekh and Lisa Marie Pepe

Divya Parekh is an award-winning business relationship advisor, international speaker and 5-time #1 International bestselling author and a writing muse who has had great success with aspiring authors, consultants, trainers, leaders, entrepreneurs, and speakers. Divya's books and strategies have been endorsed by the likes of Brian Tracy, Marshall Goldsmith, Kevin Harrington ("Shark Tank"), James Malinchak (ABC's "Secret Millionaire"), Sherry Winn (two-time Olympian) and many more….

Divya brings her business expertise and success as an author together to guide others in the writing, publication, and marketing of books that will enhance their professional credentials and propel their business to new heights.

The foundation of Divya's success is that any professional or entrepreneur can achieve their highest goals by building and nurturing relationships. She has helped many people create a thriving business that is joyful and easy to run. Her philosophy when it comes to launching books and careers is that it is all about hearts and hugs—how much you impact and help people with your life and your work!

Divya supports both first time and published authors to turn their unique message into an inspiring movement. She does this by helping them communicate their message through business-focused and personalized book writing. This approach, in turn, positions them as an industry leader, accelerates business growth and increases business profits. Divya's best-selling books, including her newest #1 Bestseller, *The Entrepreneur's Garden – The Nine Essential Relationships to Cultivate Your Wildly Successful Business*, proves that her concepts reap huge rewards.

As a professional certified coach who has helped multi-million-dollar entrepreneurs, seasoned executives, and non-profit leaders from six continents, Divya is actively working with authors with the same passion. Her proven success strategies have resulted in her clients getting six-figure opportunities, five-figure promotions, media recognition, and to the #1 bestseller list on Amazon.

Please accept my Free Gift:
"Get Started in A Week-Business Book Writing" Challenge

Friends, I get a lot of great questions from clients and people about how to get started to write a book in a faster way — without adding stress and a ton of extra hours to their plate. The questions arise because 81% of people have a book in them. Few ever finish. If you believe that you have a message that will impact others, then I know that your book is needed. Many people are doing things in a way that are…cumbersome, time-consuming, overwhelming and more complicated than they need to be. So, I've decided to create a *No-Cost and Low Effort 5 Day Challenge* to help you, a person who wants to share their message, make an impact as well as amplify profits.

Join the few and become an author. It's not that hard. I'll walk you through it in a simple, five-day "Get Started in A Week-Business Book Writing" Challenge at your pace and in comforts of home.

https://success.divyaparekh.com/5daywritingchallenge

Lisa Marie Pepe is The Confidence Coach and Online Visibility Expert for passionate, heart-centered women entrepreneurs, a #1 International best-selling author of *The Art of Unlearning: Top Experts Share Conscious Choices for Empowered Living*, and a motivational speaker.

Trained at the graduate level in both Education and Clinical Psychology and with over three years of experience as a successful virtual assistant and social media manager, Lisa Marie empowers her clients to fully embrace their unique gifts and talents by providing them with the skills they need to develop rock-solid confidence and become vibrantly visible online.

She has been featured in *The Huffington Post*, *Thrive Global*, *YFS*, and several other noteworthy publications. Lisa Marie has also appeared as a special guest expert on over 40 international telesummits and has been interviewed on dozens of highly regarded podcasts such as The Stellar Life, The Big Movement, and Women in Leadership.

Lisa Marie is available to speak on self-empowerment, overcoming obstacles, confidence building, positive psychology, entrepreneurship, online business growth and development, and online visibility strategy.

Please accept my Free eBook:

6 Ways to Amplify Your Online Visibility

In this guide, you'll receive step by step instructions, tips, tricks, and strategies on how to best: Share Your Social Media Links Be Consistent and Congruent on Social Media Use Customized Hashtags on All Your Posts Repurpose Your Facebook Livestreams Optimize Your Facebook Business Page Use Automated Response Apps ... all so that you can AMPLIFY YOUR ONLINE VISIBILITY!

https://positivetransformationlifecoaching.leadpages.co/6-ways/

www.ingramcontent.com/pod-product-compliance
Lightning Source LLC
LaVergne TN
LVHW051844080426
835512LV00018B/3070